Understand Financial Risk in a Day

Alex Kiam

TAKE THAT LTD.

TTL

Take That Ltd.
P.O.Box 200
Harrogate
HG1 2YR
Fax: 01423-526035
Email: sales@takethat.co.uk

**You should take independent financial
advice before acting on material
contained in this book.**

Printed and bound in Great Britain.

ISBN 1-873668-24-4

Contents

For Strife

Other books in the *Understand in a Day* series:

Understand **Derivatives** in a Day, by Stefan Bernstein
Understand **Bonds & Gilts** in a Day, by Ian Bruce
Understand **Shares** in a Day, by Ian Bruce

Chapter 1

Risk and Exposure

R ISK IS ONE of those words which are easy to define but not so easy to understand. And nowhere is this problem more pronounced than in the financial world. Put simply, risk is a chance of suffering a loss or being exposed to misfortune. So, extending this to money management, you can define "financial risk" as:

> *Financial risk is the chance of exposure*
> *to monetary loss.*

In an effort to understand the true meaning of risk it is best, perhaps, to break it down into "uncertainty" and "exposure to that uncertainty".

Take, for example, the case of a bungee jumper standing on a bridge contemplating his first jump. He is faced with some uncertainty. There is a chance that the rope will break and he will fall to his death below, or it will be too long and he will be dashed on the rocks. But so long as he stays on the bridge, that uncertainty remains purely hypothetical.

Only by jumping is he exposing himself to that uncertainty and creating a risk; if events go against him he will suffer personally. However the act of jumping off the bridge has not changed the actual uncertainty (as to the integrity or length of the rope).

You could also consider an observer on the bridge, watching the jumper hurl himself off the edge. They also have the same uncertainty. But because they are not making the jump themselves they are not exposed to that uncertainty and face no risk.

This illustrates quite clearly how two individuals, when facing the same uncertainty, are taking on different levels of risk. Of course this is a simplified example and risk exposure is rarely so black and white. For example the observer may be a relative of the person about to jump. Should the rope fail and the jumper be killed then the relative would suffer emotionally. Alternatively the observer could be the insurer of the bungee jumper, who would suffer financially in the event of an accident.

You can see from all of this that your assessment of risk, and hence the way in which you deal with that risk, is highly personal. It is also dependent on your knowledge or ignorance of certain facts. For example, the bungee jumper may be a regular on the bridge and could have made hundred of jumps before. In this case he would have less uncertainty about the risks involved.

The next person in line, however, may be a virgin jumper and have no knowledge of what to expect. So it could be said that the experienced jumper is taking less of a risk than the newcomer.

Financial Risk

To further emphasise how risk is essentially personal, let's take the example of two investors A and B. Both are considering buying shares in The Black Gold Oil Exploration

Company. They have done their research and acquired the latest company reports along with details of a big oil find. However the shares have proven volatile in the past, so both A and B realise they are taking a financial risk. On the surface it appears both investors are facing the same uncertainty. However, investor B is actually a chemical engineer and, having read the production figures in the report, realises the Company's profits could be boosted substantially in the short term. He will therefore believe that he is taking less of a risk buying the shares than investor A.

In an alternative scenario, though, investor A may be a petroleum engineer who looks at the oil viscosity and concludes that it may be difficult to get out of the ground, making the field less viable. In this case B's knowledge of the production figures leads him to think he is taking less risk than A when in fact he is taking a lot higher risk. A classic case of a little knowledge being a dangerous thing.

The only difference between the two investors who have access to the same facts is their knowledge. And this is the first step in overcoming your potential exposures to monetary loss. Learn as much as you can about risks, understand how to measure them, and then you can set about managing your exposure.

A Different Perspective

Once you have accepted that risk is a personal experience you also need to realise that it depends on your own perspective. For example, an investor in a company is primarily concerned with its share price and movement. The financial director of the same company may see his main risks as those of rising interest rates or the spiralling cost of raw materials. Both have an avid interest in the profitability of the company and will see the same rewards in the shape of share price movement. However they will experience different worries along the line.

To complicate matters, the same risk can generate different outcomes for each individual. For example, one of the risks faced by the financial director of the above company was interest rates - or interest rate risk. The company may be taking on a new contract and need to borrow heavily in order to meet production schedules. If interest rates rise during the period of the new loan the company will suffer monetary loss over and above that which they would have experienced if interest rates had stayed steady.

In another scenario, the same company may have enough capacity to fulfill the new order without extra investment and may receive a hefty deposit from their new customer. In this case the company will only suffer relative monetary loss if interest rates were to fall.

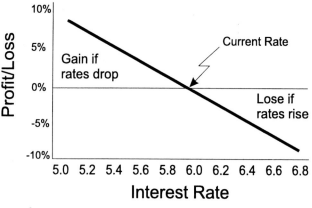

Figure 1

The overall picture for financial institutions is even more complex. At any one time banks will have large deposits from some customers whilst making equally big loans to others. The interest rates on those loans and deposits may be fixed or floating, and the funds may be in a foreign currency. At the same time they may be making investments on behalf of their clients or even helping to set certain market rates. In short, they are facing large scale exposure to all financial risks, almost all of the time.

What does all of this tell us? Risk is an uncertainty and an exposure to that uncertainty. It is personal. And it depends to a large extent on your understanding of a subject and the perspective from which you are approaching it. In other words:

Financial Risk, and the treatment of it,
is highly subjective!

Nevertheless, we need to make a start somewhere - after all, ignorance is one of our main enemies. So a helpful start can be made by splitting an overall risk into two active parts; market risk and specific risk. Attempts can then be made to measure those risks before taking steps to manage them and avoiding monetary loss.

Specific Risk

This term is used to describe the risks associated with a particular company and that company alone, or a specific financial instrument.

For example, take an investment in a baby food manufacturer. Say there is a mix up at the factory and some food stuffs become contaminated. The company will need to take drastic measures which may include national advertising, withdrawing their products from supermarket shelves, and refunding individuals who already have the product. They may also need to close their factory while investigations take place and their procedures are corrected. There will undoubtedly be a lot of negative coverage in the media and the company's image will take a battering. Profits in the short term and perhaps in the medium term will be hit and the share price will fall correspondingly. To add to their financial woes the company may be fined and, with their reputation tarnished, could face a higher cost of money from their lenders.

In this situation it is just one baby food manufacturer who has suffered and others in the same sector will not be affected. Indeed, their main competitors may benefit from the problems by way of increased market share.

Market Risk

This is a risk associated with the field in which a company acts or in which a financial instrument is traded. All companies or instruments in the same market will be affected by an unpredictable event.

For example, a TV documentary may expose dangerous ingredients in a form of baby milk. Sales across the country will drop and all companies will be affected. Their profits will decline and their investors will sell shares as the entire sector becomes depressed. It will take time to recover from the effects and there may be some casualties along the way. Therefore institutions will be less keen to lend to the sector and money supply will become more expensive.

Summary

- Risk is created by an uncertainty and an exposure to that certainty.

- Risk is personal since it depends on an understanding or ignorance of facts.

- Risk is also subjective because an individual's perspective can change with time.

- Financial risks can be broken down into market risk and specific risk.

- Specific risk is associated with a particular company or financial instrument.

- Market risk is associated with the field/sector in which a company acts or a financial instrument is traded.

Once financial risk has been identified there is a need to overcome or manage it. This can be achieved by:

1) Creating a portfolio and diversifying,

2) Predicting the movement of markets as closely and as accurately as possible,

3) Using financial instruments to hedge your risks.

But before you decide exactly how to tackle the financial risks that you are facing it is wise to quantify and to qualify those risks. So you will first need to find a way of measuring the risks involved.

Chapter 2

Financial Risk Models

THERE IS little doubt that modern portfolio theory was introduced to the world by **Harry Markowitz** in the 1950's. He published a series of papers on "*Portfolio Selection*" which were the first to formalise and quantify the idea of diversification and its application to financial instruments.

The main points of his model were:-

- The overall portfolio risk is less than the weighted average of the individual risks.

- The portfolio risk will be lower the more diversified the assets.

- The risk of an individual asset can be thought of consisting of two parts. One which can be diversified away and made to "disappear". And the other part which will always be present and will have to be carried by the investor.

As a result of Markowitz formulations, selecting a portfolio is reduced to the simple task of maximising returns whilst at the same time minimising risks.

Diversification

These days even the smallest investor is introduced to the principal diversification at an early stage as a way of managing risk.

In an earlier example we discussed the possibility of one single baby food manufacturer facing problems and as a result its share price dropping. In this instance, if an investor had put his entire savings into that company he would have been very badly hit. Yet, in accordance with the first main principal of Markowitz's work, if the same investor had placed his savings into shares of several baby food manufacturers his exposure to the manufacturing problems would have been less and his financial loss would have been smaller.

So you can see that despite the risk of disruptive plant problems being the same for any one baby food manufacturer, the overall risk of the portfolio is less (since all manufacturers are unlikely to suffer from the same production problems at the same time).

However, in the second example the entire sector was affected by adverse media comment. In this situation even the portfolio which had been diversified to several baby food manufacturers would have been hit.

Here you can see the second of Markowitz's principals in action. The assets in the portfolio are somewhat related by virtue of them all being in the same sector. As a result the overall risk of the portfolio is higher than if the assets had been chosen from various other sectors. If the portfolio had been constructed of shares in companies from the banking world, oil exploration, telecommunications and water then the risk (in this case to the food scare) would have been less.

How far you can take diversification is an interesting problem. If your portfolio is constructed from shares in every single sector then you have reduced specific risk a long way, but you are still exposed to the market risk. So, if your shares were all in British companies and the Footsie dropped, you would expect your portfolio to follow at the same rate. The next step would be to diversify into overseas markets, but even these are becoming more integrated and carry with them a new risk - that of currency risk.

The Efficient Frontier

If you are starting from scratch and creating a new portfolio you can try to optimise it in one of two ways:-

1. You can choose an expected return on your investment and consider all possible portfolios with that expected return. Then, from all of those portfolios, you select the one which has the lowest risk.

2. You choose a level of risk which you will accept and consider all the possible portfolios which have that level of risk. Then, again, you select the one which has the highest expected return.

Whichever route you choose you will produce a set of **optimal portfolios**. Route 1 will produce an optimal portfolio for each expected return. Whilst Route 2 will produce an optimal portfolio for each level of risk. The two sets will be exactly the same and together they are called the **Efficient Frontier** - shown more graphically in Figure 2.

This is a typical Efficient Frontier shown in "Risk Return Space". The region to the left of the Frontier is unobtainable and no portfolio can be constructed which can give returns in this region (for example you cannot achieve a 15% expected return by accepting a risk of only 5%). For every point to the right of the curve, however, there is at least one portfolio which can be made from all possible investments that has an expected return and risk corresponding to that point.

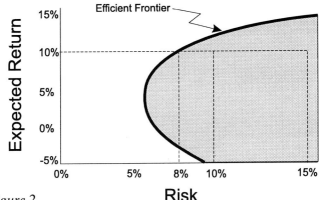

Figure 2

Consider for example an expected return of 10%. Drawing a line across the graph you can see that a portfolio with a risk of 15% could be constructed to give such a return. Similarly, you could construct a portfolio with a risk of 10% to give the same return. However your aim, surely, is to minimise the risk that you are facing. So your target must be to construct a portfolio with a risk of 8% which will also give you an expected return of 10%. This portfolio lies on the Efficient Frontier and is the best or optimal portfolio for an expected return of 10%.

Typically the portfolio which lies on the Efficient Frontier (corresponding to a risk of 8%) will be the one which is most highly diversified. All the portfolios to the right of this frontier will tend to be less diversified and show increasing levels of inter-relation.

Along with his three main principals, Markowitz established the idea that any single financial instrument should not be evaluated on its own. Indeed the contrary is true, and the attractiveness or not of an asset will depend to a large extent of the contribution it makes to the whole portfolio. Unfortunately, however, Markowitz's approach requires exact knowledge of the value of all the assets that are being considered, along with volatility data (a measure of how much the value varies over time) and correlation factors with the other assets in the portfolio. As a result the model runs into big problems when there are a large number of assets involved.

Capital Asset Pricing Model

The next big breakthrough for financial risk modelling came in the early part of the 1960's when James Tobin and Bill Sharpe designed the Capital Asset Pricing Model (CAPM). This model extended the portfolio diversification principal from the previous decade, whilst simplifying some of the assumptions regarding means, standard deviations, correlations and the like. On the downside CAPM assumes a simplified financial world where there are not taxes or dealing costs, where all investors share identical investment aims, and where they also have identical perceptions regarding expected returns and the risks involved.

CAPM starts by dividing the risk of holding assets into market risk and specific risk, as discussed earlier. **Market risk** is associated with "the movement of the market" as a whole where each individual investment is affected to a similar extent. **Specific risk**, on the other hand, is unique to an individual investment. It represents that part of an asset which is volatile and is totally uncorrelated to the general market movement.

According to the CAPM *financial markets will compensate investors for taking market risk but not for taking on specific risk*. This is because specific risk can be diversified away and no one should expect to be compensated for carrying an unnecessary risk.

As an investor you will inherently not like the idea of risk in your portfolio, and would expect the prospect of a good return before you will take it on. So, because market risk cannot be avoided, you will expect a higher return for your exposure to the market risk. In the CAPM this market risk is measured using "beta".

Beta

Imagine, for the moment, there is a way of investing that carries absolutely no risk whatsoever. This will give you a certain return and there is absolutely no way that it will be higher or lower. Of course, such an investment does not exist, but something like treasury bills (government bonds with a maturity of less than a year) come very close.

Now imagine any other portfolio. By definition it is going to have some form of risk associated with it. As an investor you do not like the idea of risk, so to take it on you will require a higher return than the risk free investment. The difference between the **risk free interest rate** and the rate that you require on your risk portfolio is known as the **"excess return"**.

For example if you were investing in a portfolio of equities which is being diversified to include every possible equity in the market, then you are still taking on a risk over and above that of investing in treasury bills. So you will require an incentive in the form of an excess return, or in this case an equity risk premium.

Alternatively you may have decided to invest in a portfolio of precious metals. Expand your portfolio and diversify it to include an investment in every possible precious metal in the market. Now you are carrying the risk that the price of precious metals across the board will drop. So you will be requiring an excess return or risk premium for investing in metals in the first place.

Such market risks are measured using "beta". It is defined as:-

$$\textbf{Beta} = \beta = (\sigma_p \times \sigma_{p,m}) / \sigma_m$$

Where σ_p is the return volatility of the portfolio, σ_m is the return volatility of the market, and $\sigma_{p,m}$ is their correlation values. The expected excess return for your portfolio above the risk free rate is simply your portfolio's beta multiplied by the expected excess return of the market portfolio.

Put into the form of words, beta is measuring the tendency of your portfolio to participate in general market moods. So a portfolio with a beta of 1.0 will tend to move roughly in line with that of the general market.

A portfolio with a beta of 0.8 will tend to gain 8% for every 10% gain in the market or lose 4% for each 5% loss of the market.

Another portfolio may have a beta of 2.1 and will tend to produce results of just over twice that of the market. If the market rises by 10% your portfolio should rise by 21%. If, on the other hand the market drops by 10% your portfolio should drop by 21%.

Portfolios with betas of around 0.5 or less would be described as defensive positions. Whereas those with a beta of two or more would generally be described as aggressive or risky.

Calculating an Excess Expected Return

To calculate the excess expected return for a portfolio we need to return to the Capital Asset Pricing Model. More fully this is expressed as:

$$E(R_p) = R_f + \beta[E(R_m) - R_f]$$

Where R_f is the risk free rate, $E(R_p)$ is the expected return on the portfolio, and $E(R_m)$ is the expected return on the market.

Say you have a defensive portfolio of equities where the market risk premium has been shown historically to be around 8%. The beta of your portfolio is 0.3 and the real interest rates are 4.0%. Your required excess return for this portfolio would be equal to 6.4% (4.0 plus 0.3 x 8.0).

If you have an aggressive portfolio with a beta of 2.2 and the same real interest rate, your expected excess return would be a massive 21.6% (4.0 plus 2.2 x 8.0).

You can see that it is easy to use beta as a measure of a portfolio's risk. However this is only really appropriate for a very highly diversified portfolio where market risk is by far and away the major source of risk. For less diversified portfolios, and this includes the majority of investors, be they individuals or institutions, specific risk is more significant and should not be ignored. For these portfolios it would be totally misleading to use beta as a measure of total risk and could yield disastrous results.

What is more, if the Capital Asset Pricing Model could be applied to smaller portfolios or single assets all you would

ever need to know would be its beta with respect of the
market portfolio. This is clearly not the case and you
would not expect to model something as complex as asset
risk based on one simple variable. Instead you need to
take note of the characteristics of all the risks involved and
model them appropriately.

Whilst this is inherently more complex it is being made
possible by the use of powerful computers in the modern
financial world.

Multiple Factor Models

A generalisation of the Capital Asset Pricing Model was
developed in 1976 by Ross in the *Journal of Economic
Theory* which he called the **Arbitrage Pricing Theory**.
It uses less assumptions and allows for multiple risks together
with the associated excess returns required for an individual
instrument.

It is written mathematically as:-

$$R_t = B.f_t + E_t$$

Where R_t is a vector of the individual assets excess returns in
period t; B is a matrix of exposures to different risk factors, f_t
is a vector of individual factor risk premia in period t, and E_t
are the individual assets' residual returns over the same period t.

This may look complex, and indeed it is. A full explanation of
the mathematics behind it is beyond the scope of this book but
is not actually necessary. Suffice to say that it has a similar
form to the CAPM, but each of the factors involved are made
up of "matrices". A matrix is only a way of writing several

things at the same time and appears to look like a table with rows and columns. The more factors that are involved the more rows and columns there will be in the matrix. A vector, as described in the equation above, is a matrix with just one row or just one column. The more risks you wish to consider for your assets or investments the larger the matrices will become and the more complex the calculations will be.

Although multiple risk factor models are now widely accepted in the financial world, the equation given above does not give a way to establish individual risk factors. Instead you need to rely on observation of historical data and back out the individual factors from the data. There are essentially three ways that you can do this, with:-

> ✔ Fundamental factor models
> ✔ Macroeconomic factors
> ✔ Statistical models

Fundamental Factor Models

This group of models assumes that B in the arbitrage pricing theory model is known and hence real data for R_t and E_t will give an estimate of f_t. In short it involves watching what investment managers and financial analysts do and assuming that their decisions bear a relation to the exposures of different risk factors (which is, after all, their job). It avoids the fact that you cannot create a full list of asset exposures to risk factors, but it is generally assumed that these include well known values such as:-

> ● Interest rate sensitivity,
> ● Price earnings ratio,
> ● Liquidity,

- Dividend yield,
- Earnings growth,
- and, exchange rate sensitivity.

Using these factors for B it is possible to back out from your observations if there was a risk premium f_t associated with each of those risks.

If an important risk is left out of set B then not only will a risk premium, f_t, not be associated with it, but all of the other risk premia will be skewed.

Nevertheless fundamental factor models are currently the most widely used methods for estimating risks.

Macroconomic Factor Models

These models take the opposite approach to fundamental factor models. Instead of assuming B and estimating ft, they assume ft and calculate B. Similarly instead of trying to draw up a full list of risk exposures, this time you need to create a list of macroeconomic events that will have an impact on the present value and return of the investment.

It assumes that expected events are already included in the price of an asset and it is only unexpected changes which require a risk premium. Of course a full list of unexpected changes is totally impossible to create, since, after all, they are "unexpected". However the following are generally assumed to be the most important:-

- Changes in interest rate
- Changes in inflation
- General investor confidence
- Overall industrial production

Now by observing real data you are able to complete the matrix B and estimate the individual exposures to the different risk factors.

Statistical Models

These models try to simultaneously estimate B and f_t. Here there is no attempt to quantify the nature of the risk premium or the factor sensitivities involved at all. Instead they seek to summarise risk by creating a probability distribution for an uncertain event and summarise that distribution with one or more statistics. They have the advantage that they can summarise an entire probability distribution but a downside that they have no real economic interpretation. This, in turn, brings in subjective view points which economic models seek to remove in the first place.

The methodology behind statistical risk measure models are often hard to follow. It is, perhaps, for this reason that they are the least popular of the three classes of multiple factor models.

Benchmarking

All risks are relative. You could say that jumping out of an aeroplane with a parachute strapped to your back is a risky adventure. And it certainly does expose you to a higher risk of death than sitting in your armchair at home reading a good book. However it is considerably less risky than jumping out of aeroplane *without* a parachute.

And the same applies in the financial world. Taking a punt on the Italian Lira could be considered more risky than investing in Deutchmarks. However it would be considered as a safe haven along side the risks associated with Bolivian Pesos, for example.

So to have real meaning any discussion of risk should first identify a zero level or neutral point. The choice of this neutral point will depend on the portfolio manager, whether they be an individual investor or the head of a huge pension fund. And it then becomes their job to increase the value of their portfolio over and above that of the agreed benchmark.

For example an individual may construct a portfolio with the aims of producing better returns than he could by putting the same amount of money into his bank account. Alternatively he may have a friend who has been investing in the stock market for a while and set himself the aim of out performing their portfolio. Creating a portfolio to out perform a bank account would not necessarily mean taking on a large amount of risk. Whereas the friend may already have a portfolio constructed mostly of equities, so the investor would expect to need a portfolio containing more risky investments than his friend on the basis that it is risk that is rewarded.

In both cases the only measure of the investor's success will be the value of his portfolio at the end of a set period compared to the notional value of investing in a bank or in the same investment as his friend. If, at the end of the year, his portfolio has out performed a bank account he will be happy. But if a portfolio shows a lower return than could have been achieved in a bank account, after having taken on a larger amount of risk, the investor would not be too pleased. However, if the same investor had set his benchmark as "beating his friend", then it is irrelevant what a bank account may have done. He may have significantly out performed a bank deposit account with his portfolio, but if he has failed in the objective of beating his friend then the end result is one gloomy investor.

Financial institutions, of course, take a broader view. Here a fund manager may set their benchmark as, say, the FTSE-100 or the S&P-500. If, at the end of the year, the manager can show that their portfolio has out performed the FTSE-100 or the S&P-500 then the fund owner will be happy - and more likely to give the manager a whacking great bonus! This does not necessarily mean the fund has to show a large monetary gain. Obviously if the FTSE-100 rises by 10% and the fund manager's portfolio rises by 15% then everyone is happy. But should the FTSE-100 have a bad year and drop by 10% then the fund manager and the owner will still be happy if their portfolio has only dropped by 5% in real terms.

It is this out-performance of a benchmark by fund managers, through the acceptance of risk, that creates their worth. After all, why should anybody be rewarded for producing the same results as a market portfolio?

Value At Risk

Whereas private individuals and fund managers are concerned with the performance of their portfolio relative to their benchmark over a period of a year or so, other financial players such as market makers, brokers and corporate treasurers are concerned with much shorter time intervals. This obviously makes it impossible for them to use an index such as the FTSE-100 as a meaningful test of their exposure to risk. Instead the only viable option for them is to compare their efforts to the returns which could be achieved by putting their money on deposit. Their aim, therefore is to make more money (or lose less) than they could through the deposit route.

An appropriate risk measured for this activity is known as "*Value At Risk*" (VAR), which directly quantifies how much money can be made in a pre-defined period. This VAR is a statistical risk measure used for a stated period and a given confidence level. For example the definition of value at risk, for a one week period, measured at a 95% confidence level, would be:-

The amount of money that an investment is expected to make more than the same amount of money 95 weeks out of 100.

So a portfolio with a one-week, 95% confidence value at risk of £10 million would be expected to make more than £10 million over 95 weeks out of 100. Similarly a portfolio with a one-day, 99% confidence value at risk of £5,000 would be expected to make more than £5,000 over 99 days out of 100.

Index Trackers

Portfolios constructed in such ways as to track a particular index have become very popular over the last few years. Their aim is to follow the movements of a particular index as closely as possible so that, at any time, they are neither ahead or behind the benchmark. Obviously they are classed as defensive.

The construction of indices such as the FTSE-100, FTSE mid-250, FT All-share, and FTSE Eurotrack-100 are all well known as well as the way they are updated. The same applies to indices from mature markets such as the USA and European Union down to the developing economies of Asia and Latin America. The aim of the index tracking portfolio is to replicate as closely as possible the construction of the index over a given period.

However, exact replication is impossible. This is because all indices are dynamic with their compositions changing as components grow, decline or merge. To take these changes into account all indices are re balanced periodically. In an attempt to keep pace with these changes an index tracking portfolio will encounter transaction costs which need to be taken out of the body of the portfolio. Sometimes these may prove too large for a small change in the construction of the index (so the portfolio is not changed).

Also it may prove impossible to buy some shares in the volumes necessary to mimic the theoretical index. A recent example of this took place in the UK where several large building societies converted into banks. Many of these new banks were immediately included in the FTSE-100. Yet insufficient private investors, who had been given "windfall" shares in the new banks upon conversion, chose to sell. As a result, fund managers found themselves 'short' in the banking sector which chased prices up to a level which made them too high to justify for some portfolio's overall performance.

> *Aside: An interesting aspect of financial risk arises when a good index tracking portfolio has been put together. You can see from the above discussion that it is immensely difficult getting a portfolio together with the exact number of shares at the right price to match the original index. But imagine for a moment you have been able to do so and you have built a portfolio that exactly matches, say, the FTSE 100. Now, what do you do if you hear of impending bad news for one of the stocks? Do you temporarily sell the stock and hope to buy it back in the market later? Do you let the fall make its full impact or do you try to insure yourself against the feared market downturn?*

Given that it is virtually impossible to exactly replicate an index, the fund manager aims to keep the difference or "tracking error" down to a minimum.

Tracking Error

Tracking error is a direct reflection of the active risk inherent in a particular portfolio. It is a quantification of how different the investments are to the accepted benchmark and directly reflects a portfolio manager's approach.

An aggressive portfolio manager whose aim is to significantly out perform the benchmark will go for a large tracking error. They will use different investments to the market portfolio and take on more active risk in an attempt to create larger excess returns.

Less aggressive portfolio managers will stick as closely as possible to the benchmark and keep their active risk to a minimum. It is not uncommon for the most aggressive managers to show a tracking error in excess of 10%, while conservative portfolio managers will usually opt for a tracking error of 2% or less.

It is usually the tracking error which is used to sell a particular fund to an investor. How often do you open the pages of the financial press to see a fund or an investment portfolio bragging about how much better it has done than the average fund in its sector or that sector's accepted benchmark? Comments such as *"best performing emerging market fund for the last three years"* shows that fund manager must have accepted a larger tracking error from the accepted emerging market index - such as the Barings Securities Emerging Market Index - than the other emerging market fund managers.

Ways of adding risk to enhance a portfolio's value split, essentially, into two methods:-

- By choosing different stocks or investments to the benchmark, or
- Changing those stocks or investments at different times to the benchmark changes.

This is where individual attitudes to risk come into play and shows a portfolio managers' style. Few go in for timing the markets because it is very risky. You either get it right or wrong! Instead they concentrate on constructing a portfolio with a beta less than or greater than one by:-

- Holding larger quantities of favoured stocks
- Over weighting the portfolio in a particular sector
- Choosing high numbers of stocks or investments with particular characteristics such as low P/E ratios, high yields, etc.

Typical Tracking Errors

Portfolio Type	Typical Tracking Error (%)
Index Fund	½ -1
Blue Chip Fund	2-4
Income Fund	4-6
Growth Fund	5-7
Small Companies	8+
Recovery/Opportunity	10+

Model Risk

There is an inherent risk which needs to be added to the use of any model. And this is simply that it may be the wrong model applied at the wrong time!

Wrong Model

Many years ago, our forefathers believed that the Earth was the centre of the Universe. The Sun and all the other planets were assumed to travel around the Earth in a giant circle. Anyone simply looking up into the sky, and feeling that they weren't moving would accept it as a very good model for the Universe.

Then some astronomers set about observing the movements of the Sun and planets. From their calculations, there was no way the planets could be moving around the Earth on a circular orbit. So they added small circles onto each planet's main circular orbit. This made the observational data fit the new model and everyone was happy.

But, of course, more accurate telescopes came along and astronomers realised the planets didn't actually move in circles within circles. No, they moved in circles, within circles, within circles!! And so it went on, until one bright spark suggested the basic model was wrong and the Earth wasn't at the centre of the Universe (and free-thinkers everywhere, who have risked their jobs by questioning fundamental corporate models, can take comfort from the fact it nearly cost him his life).

Turning back to financial risk. You may choose to use the fundamental factor model to estimate your exposure to risk because you consider market capitalisation, asset liquidity, etc as being the main factors affecting your portfolio. However it may well be the case that you should really be looking more closely at factors such as changes in inflation and interest rates. In this case you would have been better off using a macroeconomic model than a fundamental factor model.

Wrong Time

An institution may have used one model successfully for a number of years. But a new set of circumstances may come along which make it no longer valid. When the model was created, for example, a bank may have been only exposing itself to risk in the bond markets. A few years on, however, it may have started dabbling in the equity derivatives market and continued to apply the same risk measures as it has always done. Unless somebody spots the error in the risk model then that bank will almost certainly head for disaster.

Volatility

Volatility is one of the most popular and basic statistical measures of risk. The reason being that it can be used to measure market risk for a single financial instrument, a group of instruments or even an entire portfolio.

It may be hard to believe but there were times, and not so long ago, that the world's financial markets were a relatively stable place. For example interest rates in Britain were fixed at 2% for nearly five years just after the second world war. Even after this, when Labour's policy of cheap money faded, interest rate changes were uncommon. These days, however, small but much more frequent changes are the norm. Whereas a graph of interest rates for the 50's and 60's would look like a series of steps, these days it is beginning to smooth out into an almost continuous curve.

The word "**volatility**" can mean different things to different people. But the most common definition used in financial markets is that of "**standard deviation**". In other words the volatility of a share, option, future, portfolio, index, or any other financial instrument is proportional as to how far its value varies from the mean.

Standard deviation can be written as:

$$\textbf{Standard Deviation} = \sqrt{\textbf{E[(X-E(X))2]}}$$

Where E is the expected value - so E(X) is the expected value of X.

This can be shown graphically by creating a probability distribution for the price of an instrument. Do this by plotting the price of the instrument along the X-axis and how many times it has closed with each price on the Y-axis. Two examples are shown in Figures 3 and 4.

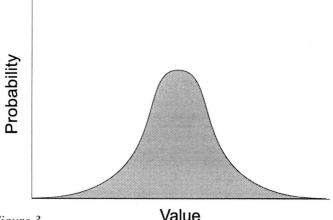

Figure 3   Value

You can see that the prices plotted in Figure 3 tend to crowd around a mean value and there is not too much of a spread. In other words the values tend to be close to the expected value and hence this probability distribution is showing a low standard deviation - this instrument would have a low volatility. The second, Figure 4, shows an instrument where the values are quite often very different from the mean value so in this case the standard deviation is high - you would say this instrument is highly volatile.

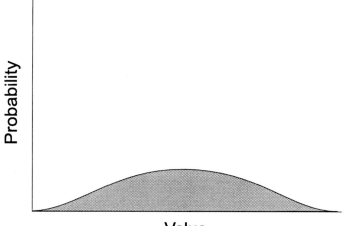

Figure 4 **Value**

If you were to plot these two instruments on a time axis graph, in other words every hour or every day, then you would obtain something like Figures 5 and 6 (see over). The first graph, Figure 5, has fairly shallow peaks and troughs and the price does not vary much either side of a straight line drawn through the middle. This is a low volatility instrument and could, for example, be a plot of treasury bill returns over a couple of years.

Figure 6, however, is for a more volatile instrument and you can see large peaks and troughs either side of a line drawn through the middle. This could be a plot of the share price for a high technology stock over a year or perhaps the exercise price of a put option over a month.

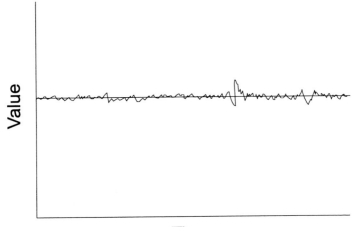

Figure 5

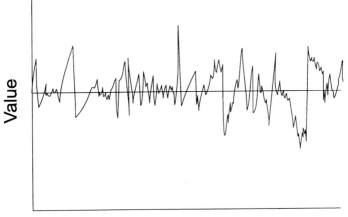

Figure 6

You will notice that the volatility of an instrument can be different depending on when you measured it. For example we have established that over a period of two, three, four or even five years a treasury bill is a low volatility instrument. But if you were to plot treasury bill returns against time for a short period when interest rates are changing rapidly (for example during sterling's ERM troubles) then you may reach the opposite conclusion and assume that they are highly volatile.

Which of these three instruments - A, B or C - would you say is the most volatile?:

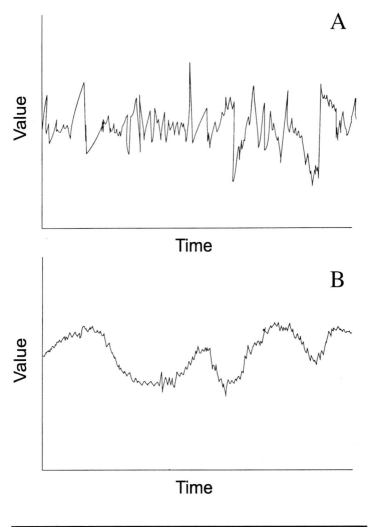

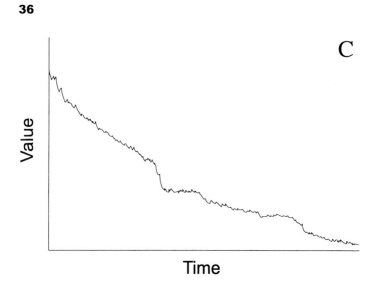

You would probably conclude that instrument A or perhaps B is the most volatile. But the real answer is that they all belong to the same instrument. The third graph is just a small section of graph B which in turn is just a small section of graph A!

Historical Volatility

There are two main methods for estimating volatility in financial markets. The first is *historical volatility* which gives an estimate based on actual market value fluctuations. In this situation you would follow a financial instrument, for example a tracking fund, and monitor its returns over, say, 365 days. By then creating a probability distribution, as discussed above, you would be able to make an estimate of the tracking fund's volatility compared to other tracking funds or indices.

This method of estimating volatility is highly flexible. It can be used for any financial instrument where historical data is readily available.

However, as you have already seen, the volatility estimated from historical data is dependent on the period under examination. Should you go for a longer sample period to obtain more data for your volatility calculation? Or should you concentrate on more recent data which could be more relevant (but not statistically more significant)?

Also, do you conclude that an instrument is not volatile if its value stays unchanged for a long time? The answer would probably be "yes", but price stability may be more a function of the instrument's liquidity than of its volatility (one which is not traded often will not change its price at regular intervals).

Finally, historical volatility may say nothing about how risky a financial instrument is now. If the historical data you have is for an option which was '*out-of-the-money*' then it would not be relevant if the same option is now '*in-the-money*'.

Implied Volatility

Historical volatility is not applicable to everybody. For traders, brokers, market makers or portfolio managers, whose positions in the market are constantly changing, historical data is virtually useless. In this situation the portfolio manager needs to know the riskiness of his portfolio as it is now (this minute, this hour, or this day) not as it was at some period in the past.

Estimates of *implied volatility* are made from option prices. Models for pricing options such as the **Black-Scholes model**, require volatility estimates to the input. So if you monitor the price of an option in the market you can use the same model to back out "implied" volatility.

Of course, implied volatility's can only be calculated if there is a large enough market in options for the financial instrument under consideration. You would have no problem, for example, calculating an implied volatility for a particular share, currency or index. But you may have problems making an estimate for local government bonds or shares in a private limited company.

The Greeks

L ater in this book options will be examined as a way of managing your exposure to risk. However all derivative instruments, such as options, introduce a new variety of risk exposures, whether they are being used as a way of managing risk themselves or as a basic part of a portfolio.

A portfolio manager may be using put and call options to hedge against risk in his portfolio but a broker, market maker or financial institution may hold them in a more speculative manor. All of these parties will want to keep their options position dynamic as they react to new information entering the market. In this situation it is not enough to know what the total risk of a portfolio's position is. Instead you will need to know what specific exposure is associated with several sources of risk; such as **changes in value of the underlying** financial instrument, **changes in volatility** of the instrument, **changes in interest rates** and, of course, **time**.

The "Greeks" are a set of factors which have been created to help describe these specific exposures. They can be applied to a particular position in the derivatives market or to an entire portfolio which include derivative instruments. They are known as the Greeks simply because they are written as Greek symbols in algebraic equations created by mathematicians to model the behaviour of options.

Delta

In (Greek) alphabetical order this is the first of the factors used to describe the risk of derivative instruments. It is a measure of the rate of change in the value of the underlying financial instrument. And since it is the change in the underlying instrument that is a primary source of risk to any portfolio containing options it is, perhaps, the most important of the Greeks.

Unfortunately changes in option price as a result of changes in the underlying instrument are not simple. They take the form of a curve as shown in Figure 7.

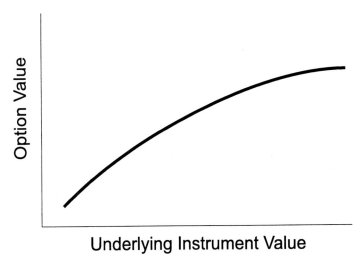

Underlying Instrument Value

Figure 7

You can see that this is not a linear relationship so, mathematically, it requires two factors (at least) to describe its behaviour. These two factors are Delta and Gamma. Delta (Δ) represents the first-order effects on the sensitivity graph. In other words it is the slope of the curve which is the most important information to an options holder. Mathematically it can be described as:

$$\textbf{Delta} = \Delta = \Delta P / \Delta U$$

Where ΔP is the change in option or portfolio value, and ΔU is the change in value of the underlying instrument.

But graphically it can be shown as a tangent to the curve showing the sensitivity of an option to the underlying instrument:

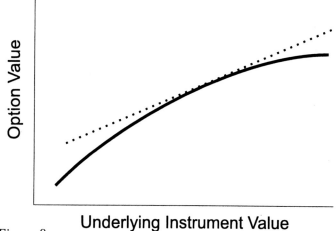

Figure 8

The Delta gives the direction and magnitude of the portfolio's sensitivity at the point where the tangential line meets the curve.

Gamma

As you can see from the above illustrations, if the sensitivity of the value of an option to changing values of the underlying instrument were linear then we would only need Delta to describe its movements. However it is not a straight line so we need to introduce a second-order coefficient. This second-order effect is described by the Greek symbol Gamma (Γ) and gives an indication as to the curvature of the option value/underlying value curve.

Essentially, instead of trying to describe the curve with a straight line, using Gamma along with Delta and a third factor which is constant, attempts to model it as a parabola. The Parabola which best fits the curve will have the mathematical description:

$$(\Gamma/2)U^2 + \Delta U + C$$

Graphically it might look something like this:

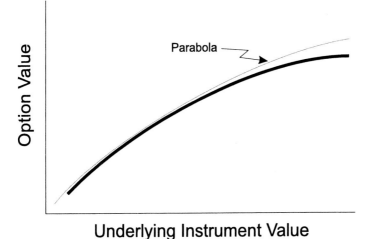

Underlying Instrument Value

Figure 9

Just as Delta told you about the direction of the slope and its magnitude, so Gamma tells you the direction and magnitude of the curvature. A positive Gamma depicts a curve which opens upwards, whilst the negative Gamma depicts one which opens downwards (see over).

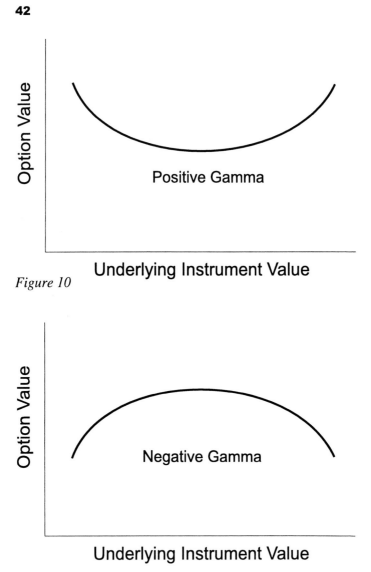

Figure 10

Figure 11

You could say that Gamma is a measure of the rate at which an option Delta is changing.

Vega

Options and other derivative instruments are sensitive to the **"implied volatility"** of the underlying instrument (for more on implied volatilities please see the Options Section under **Managing Risks**). Generally speaking, buying a position, or going long, in the Options market will benefit from rising implied volatilities and lose out from decreasing implied volatilities. Writing or selling options, going short, will show the opposite effects and lose out from rising volatilities and gain from declining volatilities.

Vega is very similar to Delta in its mathematical description. Indeed it is described by another straight line which is tangential to a curve. However this time the curve is a plot of the value of the option against implied volatility of the underlying instrument.

$$\textbf{Vega} = \varsigma = \textbf{DP/ DV}$$

Where ΔV is the change of implied volatility. Other notations for Vega include Kappa (κ), Lambda (Λ) and Sigma (Σ).

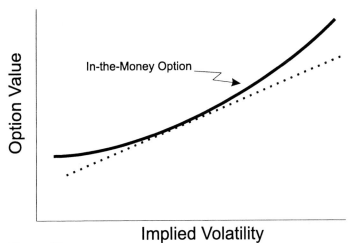

Figure 12

Rho

Just as Delta measured the sensitivity of an options value to the value of the underlying asset, and Gamma measured its sensitivity to the implied rate of interest, so Rho measures its sensitivity to interest rates. Mathematically it is defined as:

$$\mathbf{Rho} = \rho = \Delta P / \Delta R$$

Where ΔR is the change in interest rates.

Obviously interest rates affect the price of the derivative instrument because the cash that is represented in the deal could have been placed on deposit in the intervening period and would itself have increased in value. In other words it is a way of allowing for future cash flows at the present.

Theta

This is the last of the Greeks and measures a sensitivity of a derivative instrument with respect to time. In a further chapter you will see how the price of an option includes a certain "time value". An option which has been bought, a long position, will lose value as the expiry date approaches. Similarly a sold, or a short position, will gain in value. You can probably guess it, but the mathematical description of Theta is:

$$\mathbf{Theta} = \Theta = \Delta P / \Delta T$$

Where Θ is the change in time (obviously always positive!)

Summary

- The Markowitz principles and CAPM models may be nearly 40 years old but the reduction of risk by diversification is still a foundation of most investment strategies today.

- A good estimate of investment volatility and how your individual investments interact (correlation) is vital to make your risk model work.

- Accurate risk modelling is highly complex.

- Probably the best way to overcome this complexity is to estimate your risk by watching the market. In theory the overall market movement will be a result of a total knowledge of all the professionals in the market and constitutes the best risk forecast you can get. So by observing the movement of prices you will be able to back out risks involved in your portfolio through fundamental factor models.

- Investment managers, market makers, brokers, corporate treasurers and individual investors all use risk estimates in slightly different ways. Their main concern when using these estimates is how their portfolio will measure up to an accepted or pre-defined benchmark.

- The extent to which a portfolio out performs the benchmark is related to the tracking error and is important since it's used to sell a fund to a client.

Chapter 3

Forecasting

FORECASTING the movement of financial instruments from individual shares through to indices is an essential feature in the process of managing financial risk. Without a good forecast you are just leaving yourself open to chance and sooner or later you will lose out.

Imagine you are skiing towards a cliff. It does not take a genius to work out that there is a risk coming up in the near future! But without some kind of forecast as to what will happen it is very difficult to make a decision on what to do. It could be that the 'cliff' is a narrow gully and you can see a soft landing on the other side. In this case, you may decide to ski as fast as possible and jump the gully. On the other hand, it may look like a precipice and you'll brake as hard as possible.

In the financial markets you probably won't be faced with any cliff faces but you will be affected by a constant stream of new factors, some good and some bad. A good forecast of what is likely to happen outside of these pieces of news will determine how you will deal with each one as it comes along.

Your forecasting technique will be determined by your activities in the market. Some individuals, companies or institutions such as market makers, commodity dealers and brokers will take a very short term view on the market. Their buying and selling of any instruments can swing widely throughout the day and even throughout the hour. So they need a forecast as to what is likely to happen over the next few hours and days.

Other market participants such as portfolio managers are unlikely to be concerned with what happens throughout a day. Instead they are worried about the risks their portfolios face over the next three months to a year (or however often their strategic reviews take place). Unless something really important and totally unexpected happens they are likely to leave their position unchanged between reviews.

Finally there are a group who are only interested in very long term forecasts. These will include economists, corporate decision makers, and financial analysts. Their period of planning will cover several years at a time and they will devise their strategy accordingly.

There are possibly as many ways of forecasting market movements as their are people in the market. Each has his or her favourite and has possibly made their own little alterations to the original model. Broadly speaking, however, they fall into two classes, those who follow technical analysis and those who go for fundamental analysis.

Technical Analysis

Technical analysis only looks at the past history of a financial instrument and makes no attempt to establish what factors may have caused it to move in such a way. These methods are often used to establish forecasts for individuals, companies or institutions with a short to medium term interest in the market

Oscillators

These indicators are intended to provide an idea of trends in the market.

The momentum indicator is one of the most simple technical analysis equations around. It simply gives the difference between the current market price of an instrument and the price of a same instrument a certain number of days ago:

Momentum indicator = (current value - value N days ago)

The number of days, N, used will depend on your interest in the market. If the momentum indicator is high then this implies that the instrument is overbought and the forecast is for it to fall. If the momentum indicator is low then this indicates that the instrument is oversold and the forecast is for it to rise.

The Relative Strength Index (RSI) oscillates between an upper limit of 100 and lower limit of zero. If the RSI is above 70 then the market is thought to be overbought and the forecast is for a fall. If the RSI is below 30 then the market is thought to be oversold and the forecast is for a rise. It is calculated by using the following formula:

$$RSI = 100 - \left(\frac{100}{\sum (+ \text{ changes } / - \text{ changes}) + 1} \right)$$

This oscillator is preferred to the simple momentum indicator because it is normalised. Since the bounds are from 0 to 100 you can see easily if a market is considered overbought or oversold. Whereas with the momentum indicator you need to make your own decision on what is classed "high" and what is classed "low".

The Volume Accumulation Indicator (VAI) measures the trading volume against fluctuations in the price in the same instrument. The basic idea is that if the market spends most of a given period, say a day or month, moving downward and ends with an upturn, then the positive movement will be interpreted in relation to the whole period. The VAI formula is given by:

$$VA = [((MC-ML)-(MH-MC))/(MH-ML)] \times V$$

Where VA is the volume accumulation MC is the market close, ML is the market low, LH is the market high and V is the volume.

These figures can usually be obtained from the financial pages of newspapers.

Charts

This is perhaps the most popular way of forecasting the movement of a financial instrument. Users plot the movement in the price of a particular financial instrument such as a share, bond, option, future or index and then attempt to spot patterns on the graph and draw lines through trends. The chartists then use their skills to interpret signs with such exotic names as falling wedges, bearish rectangles, up-trend channels and pennants in an effort to forecast the next movement.

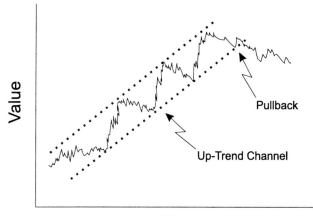

Figure 13 **Time**

Moving Average

This charting technique works on a sample of market data by creating an average over a number of days less than the total.

For example you can calculate the seven day moving average from a set of data covering eight or more days. To start you take the first seven days from the sample and calculate the average value. This is your first point on the moving average graph. Once plotted you return to the same data and drop off the first or earliest data point from your original seven leaving you with six values. To this six you now add the next piece of data in the series which will be the eighth point. You then take an average of these new seven pieces of data, 2 - 8 to give you your second point on the graph. The third graphical point will be an average of data points 3 - 9 inclusive, the fourth will be an average of 4 - 10 inclusive, etc.

Calculating a Seven-day Moving Average

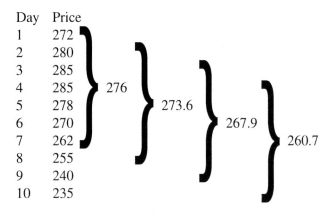

Day	Price
1	272
2	280
3	285
4	285
5	278
6	270
7	262
8	255
9	240
10	235

276   273.6   267.9   260.7

This moving average line is then superimposed on top of the original data. And where the original data lines and moving average lines cross gives an indication as to whether the instrument is likely to rise or fall. If the original data line crosses the moving average line in an upward direction the market will rise. And if the data line crossed the average line in a downwards direct, the forecast is for a fall.

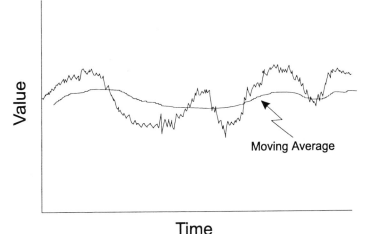

Figure 14

The Moving Average Convergence/Divergence (MACD) is a modification of the moving average chart to show divergence (or convergence) of two separate moving averages. One of these moving averages will be calculated for the short term and the other for a longer term. When the financial instrument is trending in one direction, say upwards, the shorter term moving average will rise more rapidly than the longer term moving average.

The difference between these two averages is calculated and plotted on a graph as the **oscillator line**. As this line falls below or rises above a benchmark known as the '**zero line**' it forecasts that the instrument will fall or rise correspondingly. The further the MACD moves from the benchmark zero line the stronger the trend is likely to be.

Reversals

Perhaps of major concern when considering risk is the reversal of a trend. In other words when a characteristic pattern has taken shape on the chart and the value of the financial instrument starts to deviate from that trend.

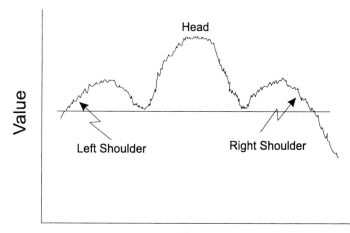

Figure 15

The head and shoulders formation is one of the most common reversal trend indicators. When drawn on a graph it appears, as the name would suggest, as a left and right shoulder with a central head which is higher than the shoulders. A neck line is drawn across the bottom of the shoulders and this is said to indicate that the value will drop once the right shoulder has been passed.

Double tops, and their inverts of double bottoms, appear something like the head and shoulders without the head. Triple tops on the other hand are like the head and shoulders trend but the peak of the head is at the same level as the shoulders. Expect also to find rounded tops and bottoms, wedge formations and island reversals! You can see the problem here is that any form of reversal can be given a name. So as the information comes in you do not really know which to follow. For example, after the second bump on the double top should you sell or hang on for a small rise on the triple top?

Support and Resistance

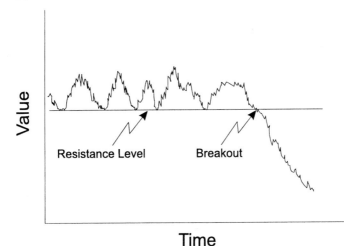

Figure 16

With these charts you attempt to find a level where the market is saying the underlying instrument does not really justify a higher (lower) price. In a rising market an instrument price may fluctuate but it will not increase above the support level. Similarly an instrument in a bear market will meet a resistance level below which its value will not fall.

The theory dictates that once the support level, or the resistance level, has been breached then there will be a sharp swing into that direction. For example, say the pound has been trading against the dollar over the last few months between $1.50 and $1.55 to the pound. The resistance level would be $1.50 below which the market is resisting a fall. The support level is obviously $1.55. Now should the pound drop below $1.50 then the chartists will say it will continue to drop further purely because it has broken this resistance level and the new trading band will be below $1.50.

You can see the problem with technical and chart analysis, from the risk point of view, is that it assumes all available information is reflected in the price of a financial instrument. Once all this information has been taken into account then the value of the instrument will behave rationally.

However risk analysis concerns itself primarily with unknown events. Obviously these can not have been reflected in any previous technical or chart movements. So when a value reaches a certain level or a trend line is broken due to some unexpected event then the whole forecast breaks down.

Fundamental Analysis

These group of forecasters attempt to find out what factors influence the value of a financial instrument. Once these factors have been identified they use their knowledge of the market in general to make a good projection for the future of that instrument.

To perform fundamental analysis properly you need to spend a large amount of time on research to establish what underlying factors make the financial instrument - share, option, index, etc - move in one direction or the other.

Accounting Ratios

These are a series methods used by analysts to extract meaningful data from company accounts. They look at items such as profitability and return on investment, the long and short term solvency of a company and the shareholders investment ratios.

Return on Capital Employed is a measure of the profitability of a company. It is calculated by dividing the profit on ordinary activities, before interest and taxation, by the full value of capital employed in the company. This ratio is then used to compare the company in question to other companies in the same sector. The higher the ROCE the better.

The debt ratio provides some measure of the financial burden carried by a company. It is defined as the ratio of the total debts to total assets. A company with a high debt ratio will be classified as more risky than one with lower ratio on the basis that the debt burden will be lower and so the cost of money to the company from banks and other institutions, will also be lower. Similar ratios include **interest cover** and **cash flow ratio**.

Share holder investment ratios are perhaps the best well known and give some indication as to a company's potential. Perhaps the most common is the **price-to-earnings Ratio** which is the company's share price divided by the earnings per share. If a company's prospects are very good then the P/E ratio will be high, and if they are poor then the P/E ratio will be smaller. P/E ratio should only be compared with companies in the same sector as a way of finding value or minimising risk. Other ratios in this category will include **earnings per share, dividend yield** and **earnings yield**.

Econometrics

This is a fairly complex area where economists are dabbling in science in an effort to quantify relationships between economic variables. It is highly theoretical and attempts to explain basic economic theory through single equations or combinations of linear equations. When all of these equations come together they would ideally explain how the whole world's economy works!

It is not surprising, considering the size of the task, that econometric models have yet to produce convincing results. The existing models explain some variations but it is accepted that they need to be modified as new relationships come to light. At this point the circles within circles attitude of ancient astronomers comes to mind!

Delphi Forecasting

Another term for this form of forecasting could be that of a "straw pole". In short you ask a lot of people who should know what they are talking about (experts in their area) for their opinions on the subject. For example you ask the heads of 10 investment houses where they think the FTSE index will end up at the end of the year. You then take a consensus of opinion from all of these experts as being the most informed forecast that you can reach. Needless to say the track records of accepted experts some times make embarrassing reading.

Summary

Forecasts of the future performance of financial instruments can be made by:

- Technical analysis using equations,
- Technical analysis using charts,
- Analysis of the economic fundamentals,
- Complex economic models,
- Straw Poles.

The problem with all of these techniques is what to do when the forecast breaks down and values move outside of those which were expected. Should you abandon your forecast, find a new one which fits the data, or start all over again?

Chapter 4

Risk Management

Forwards

ONE OF THE longest established hedging instruments are Forward contracts. They are used to manage risk primarily in the commodity and financial markets, but their simplicity makes them a favourite for non-financial enterprises as well.

> *In short, a Forward contract is an agreement between any two parties to make a deal at some point in the future. Both the date and the price at which the deal will proceed are both fixed.*

The buyer in the deal is said to be taking a **long position**, and the seller is said to be taking a **short position**. The date on which the deal will take place is the **maturity date** and the price which is fixed before hand is known as the **delivery price**.

One of the main advantages of Forward contracts is that they are termed **Over The Counter** (OTC) transactions and they can be specifically created to suit both parties. In other words the contracts are not subject to any exchanges' regulations and do not need to be in specific units of trading or mature on any specific day.

Here is an example. Say a large precision engineering company undertakes to sell engineering parts to a German car manufacturer at an agreed price of DM10 million. To clinch the deal and to help spread the risk of either party going broke, they agree that half of the contract payment should be made straight away and the other half will become due in 12 months time.

Everything is signed and the British company receives its first payment at an exchange rate of DM2.8136 to the pound; a receipt of £1,777,082. At this point the Financial Director airs his views that the company is taking on a large amount of exchange rate risk. He is aware that Germany is facing internal problems and is struggling to meet its internal financial targets. Therefore he fears that the Bundesbank will interfere in such a way as to push the Deutchmark down. Having consulted various experts in the field he concludes that at the end of the year £1 could be worth as much as DM2.9324. If this were to happen he calculates that the second payment, 12 months down the line, would only be £1,705,088, which is £71,994 less than if it was paid today.

In this situation the British company would seek to enter into a Forward contract with a financial institution. The company would be taking a short position in which they would sell Deutchmarks to the institution (long position) on the same day as the second payment would be due. So by fixing the delivery price and the delivery date with this Forward contract the company would be protected from any exchange rate movements that could occur over the next twelve months. Benchmark figures used to calculate such deals are published regularly in financial papers such as the Financial Times and Wall Street Journal. These represent a snap shot of exchange rates (interest rates, commodity prices, etc.) in the market at any one time. They are intended to give a guidance to current thinking but in highly volatile markets they could be very different to how things actually turn out. An example, relevant to the above situation, would appear like this:

Deutchmark Forward against the Pound

Spot	1 Month	3 Months	12 Months
2.8136	2.8060	2.7900	2.7197

The **spot** figure given in these tables is usually the current existing rate for immediate delivery. All the other rates are for specified intervals such as one, three and 12 months. The difference between the figures comes about as a result of different interest rates in the home markets of the different currencies (i.e. British interest rates are usually different to German interest rates). This is known as **covered interest rate parity** and the formula for calculating forward currency rates is:

$$F = S + S \times t \, (i_f - i_d)/36500$$

Where F is the forward exchange rate, S is the spot rate of the foreign currency, i_f is the risk free interest rate in the foreign country, i_d is the risk free interest rate in the domestic market and t is the number of days to maturity.

Take the Deutchmark forward against the Pound example above. When this table was published the prevailing interest rates were 6.5% in the UK and 3.0% in Germany. So inserting these figures to calculate the three month (91 days) forward rate you will calculate:

$$F = 2.8136 + 2.8136 \times 91 \times (3.0 - 6.5)/36500$$

Giving a three month forward rate for the Deutchmark against the pound of 2.7890 which is close to the 2.7900 given in the table. The same process would be used to calculate the other forward rates for one and 12 months as given in the table, or for any intervening period such as two, five or nine months.

One of the main benefits of making Forward contracts is that once made they can be forgotten. There is no need to constantly check the financial pages since the delivery date and price have both been fixed and you will know the amount you will receive or pay at maturity. So, in theory, this removes a large amount of worry from a hard working Financial Director's shoulders.

But the opposite may be true. It is possible that the market will move in the other direction. In this case the new financial risk actually comes from the Forward contract itself. For example, say one month after fixing the Forward contract the Deutchmark starts to reverse its losses and the new spot rate for the Deutchmark is DM2.7614 to the pound, and the long term trend seems to be a upwards. In this situation the British company would receive £1,810,675, which is over £33,500 more than the first payment.

Now the Financial Director is beginning to regret entering into the Forward contract with his bank. So he may seek to "unwind" his position. There are three main ways in which he could do this:-

1) If the contract terms allow he could seek to cancel the contract, but would probably incur stiff penalties.

2) He could seek to sell the contract but it would be difficult to find a buyer since, as previously indicated, Forward contracts are bespoke transactions.

3) Or he could seek to open an opposite position by taking out a new Forward contract in the other direction.

With all of these options the company will incur more costs. These include the usual institutional costs of setting up such deals as well as the cost of setting up long and short contracts at opposite ends of the usual exchange rate spread (and the bid-offer spread will depend on the financial institution's view of the company's credit worthiness).

Summary

The advantages of Forward contracts are:

  ✔ Over the counter transactions,
  ✔ Flexible amounts,
  ✔ Flexible delivery periods,
  ✔ Delivery price and date specified in the contract,
  ✔ Flexible arrangements (need not be made during an exchanges open trading times).

Disadvantages include:

  ✘ Not regulated by an exchange,
  ✘ Difficult to cancel,
  ✘ Risk of default.

Futures

Futures are essentially the same as Forwards in that it is an agreement between two parties to undertake a specific transaction at some agreed date in the future and at a price agreed now. However, the biggest single difference is that Futures Contracts are subject to the regulations of an exchange such as LIFFE (London International Financial Futures Exchange) or CME (Chicago Mercantile Exchange). These exchanges only allow deals to be made by members of the exchange which are large international financial institutions, companies or individuals who have satisfied strict joining criteria. Therefore most people wanting to deal in Futures will have to do so through a broker.

The exchange is responsible for regulating the market and running the clearing house which registers all the deals that have been struck and notes who is taking on the obligation to deliver. These activities, along with contract specification, help to ensure the integrity of the market and remove any risk of default.

Any Futures contract must conform to the specifications laid down by the exchange. These will specify fixed delivery dates and standard nominal values so that all the players in the market understand what it is exactly they are agreeing to buy or sell. A typical contract specification would look something like this:

Three Month Eurodeutschmark (Euromark)
Interest Rate Future

Unit of trading: DM 1,000,000
Delivery months: March, June, September, December plus two additional serial months such that 18 delivery months, including the three nearest calendar months, are always available for trading.
Delivery day: First business day after the Last Trading Day
Last trading day: 11.00 - Two business days prior to the third Wednesday of the delivery month
Quotation: 100.00 minus rate of interest
Minimum price movement (Tick size & value): 0.01 - DM 25
Trading hours: 07.30 - 16.10
APT trading hours: 16.25 - 17.59

Contract standard: Cash settlement based on the Exchange Delivery Settlement Price. Exchange Delivery Settlement Price (EDSP): Based on the British Banker's Association London Interbank Offered Rate (BBA LIBOR) for three month Eurodeutschmark deposits at 11.00 on the Last Trading Day. The settlement price will be 100.00 minus BBA LIBOR rounded to two decimal places. Where the EDSP Rate is not an exact multiple of 0.01%, it will be rounded to the nearest 0.01% or, where the EDSP Rate is an exact uneven multiple of 0.005%, to the nearest lower 0.01% (e.g. a BBA LIBOR of 6.12500 becomes 6.12).

The first line of this specification shows the **standard unit** of trading, which in this case is DM1,000,000. This is the value of one contract, so two contracts will be worth DM2,000,000, three contracts worth DM3,000,000, etc. It is not possible to buy any other nominal values or fractions of contracts.

The next three lines specify when delivery must take place and when contracts reach maturity.

The minimum price movement is known as a "**tick**" or a "**basis point**" and dictates the smallest price movement that is allowed for the quotation. Its value is defined by the following equation:

$$\frac{(\text{Nominal Contract Value x } 0.01)}{(100 \text{ x Number of trading periods per year})}$$

For the *Three Month Eurodeutschmark* this is:

$$(\text{DM1,000,000 x } 0.01)/(100 \text{ x } 4) = \text{DM25}$$

The last two lines tell you when the exchange is open for **normal trading** and for **automatic pit trading** (APT). You will note that these hours are quite restrictive and take very little account of time differences around the world. And this is where Forwards, which are not exchange regulated and can therefore be struck 24 hours a day, score a big plus over Futures.

The remaining specification is the quotation which is defined as:

Quotation = (100 - rate of interest)

The average person is more likely to use this formula in reverse. Quotations for *Three Months Euromark Futures* can be found in the financial pages of most quality newspapers and the table in the *Financial Times* or *Wall Street Journal* would look something like this:

Three Month Euromark Futures (LIFFE) - DM1m points of 100%

Open	Set.	Price	Change	High	Low	Est.Vol.	Open Int.
June	96.82	96.83	+0.01	96.85	96.81	20502	203563
Sep	96.76	96.79	+0.03	96.82	96.75	37630	219654
Dec	96.66	96.69	+0.04	96.72	96.65	39415	248782
Mar	96.53	96.58	+0.05	96.61	96.53	28222	232896

From this table you can see that the three month year Euromark futures which close in September are quoted at 96.76. Using the equation above you can calculate an **"implied rate of interest"** of:

$$(100 - 96.76) = 3.24\%$$

Alternatively you would calculate the implied rate of interest from a December close to be:

$$(100 - 96.66) = 3.34\%$$

Both of these implied rates of interest give you an interest rate applicable for three months on expiry of the contract. Note, however, that the interest rate implied by the price of Futures contracts will not necessarily be the same as Forward rates even if quoted on an identical basis. This is because the **Futures market is transparent** where all transactions can be observed by anyone monitoring the market. If the price of any contract varies from a "fair" quote, as perceived by the market in general, then professionals will jump into the market with the aim of making a quick buck. This activity will very quickly push the quotation back into line. On the other hand, the **Forward market is relatively opaque** and unless you are involved in particular deals you will be unaware of what interest rates are being set. The result of this difference is that the Futures market is very often used as a benchmark for the Forward market.

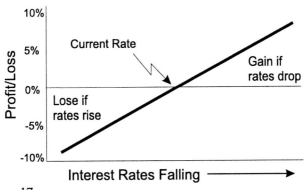

Figure 17

If you are unsure about entering into the Futures market as a way of managing your risk exposure then it is important that you find out how much demand there is for contracts over the period you are interested in. A good guide could be taken from the estimated volume as given in the quotations table. This shows how many contracts were entered into during the previous days trading. Each contract is of course worth one million Deutchmarks so you can get a feel for the weight of money following this position.

Remember, however, that Futures are traded very easily and few will be held until maturity. Indeed most contracts are arranged for speculative reasons and only very small percentage are held until delivery day. This is where the open interest figures shown in the final column comes into play. They show how many contracts with matching long and short positions are still active in the market.

Suppose a company takes out a £5 million loan in order to invest in some new machinery and move to new premises. The interest rate for the loan is set at an initial level but it is agreed that a new rate will be set every three months. Obviously if interest rates rise the company will end up paying more for its money than at the start. Similarly should interest rates fall they will see a net benefit. The risk can be illustrated graphically in Figure 17 where you will note that the X-axis shows interest rates falling to the right and rising to the left:

Now suppose the Financial Director reads the newspapers and takes the collective view that the economy is over-heating and inflation is starting to rise. He concludes that the Bank of England will raise interest rates as a way of controlling the inflation. This will lead to a higher cost of borrowing for his company and decides to hedge the interest rate risk. So he turns to the Futures market and opens a short position where he stands to gain should interest rates rise. Remembering that the price of the Future, or quotation, is given as (100 - rate of interest) you can represent this short position thus:

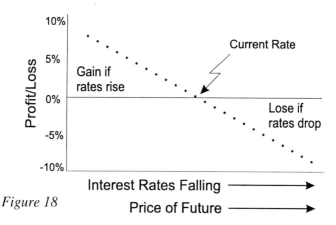

Figure 18

Superimposing the company's exposure to interest rate rises from their position in the cash market (by borrowing £5 million) and their short position in the Futures market you get Figure 19.

You can see that the Futures contract has exactly balanced the company's exposure to interest rate risk. Should interest rates rise the company will need to pay more to service its loan.

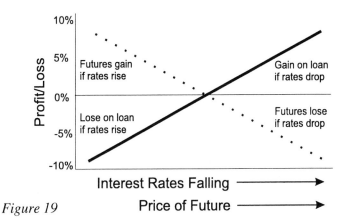

Figure 19

However, it will gain from the rise in the Futures market to the same extent. Conversely should interest rates fall the company will gain from a cheaper loan facility but lose from a fall in the Futures market.

Margin

The use of Futures as a way of managing your risk exposures would seem more attractive than the Forward market since all the transactions are regulated by an exchange and interest rates almost guaranteed to be set at a fair level. However the exchange needs to know that you are going to meet your obligations and requires a deposit, known as a "**margin**", as a way of controlling potential default.

When the contract is first arranged you will need to pay an **initial margin**. The figure for this margin will be set by the exchange and is not the final amount that you are obliged to pay. At the close of business on each day the exchange will examine every client's position in the Future's market. And if the price movements have been such that the client has lost money then the net amount is subtracted from the margin. If this margin then falls below a pre-defined level, known as the **maintenance level**, then the client is required to top up his margin account. If the market has moved in the opposite direction, however, then the client may make a withdrawal of any excess balance over the initial margin.

You will see that this requirement to deposit an initial margin and then maintain the account can work against a well hedged position. Short term movements in the market can lead to a **squeeze** of even the best designed positions and cause them to be liquidated.

Summary

The advantages of using Futures contracts are:

> ✔ Standard units of trading,
> ✔ Specified delivery dates,
> ✔ Exchange regulated market,
> ✔ Ease of buying and selling contracts through a highly liquid market.

Some of the main disadvantages are:

> ✘ Limited trading hours,
> ✘ The need to use brokers,
> ✘ The need to deposit and maintain a margin.

Swaps

Interest rate and currency swaps have been around since the early 1920's but have only become a popular tool in the financial markets since the 1980's. The swaps market is truly global and estimated to be worth more than some $2 billion

making it highly liquid. Just about every major financial institution has an interest in the market and keeps their swap book
open 24 hours a day by passing it along the financial centres.

Swaps are used as a way of controlling risk. They exist as a
result of local differences in interest rate and currency markets, as well as differing credit ratings between the companies
and institutions involved. In other words institution A may be
very well regarded in their own market but not so highly in a
market where B operates. If the opposite is true for B then
there is potential for a swap. Institution B borrows money on
behalf of institution A, allowing A to operate efficiently in B's
market. At the same time institution A borrows in its own
market on behalf of institution B, allowing B to operate in A's
market with a similar efficiency.

Swap agreements differ from the likes of Futures and Forwards in that they usually remain in force for the lifetime of a
company's exposure to a certain risk, for example until a loan
is fully repaid. So where Futures and Forwards are used as
short term instruments of perhaps three months to a year, swaps
are usually used to manage exposure for two years or more.

Interest Rate Swaps

An interest rate swap is essentially a series of forward interest
rate agreements. They are sets of contracts where two parties
agree to meet one another's interest rate payments when they
become due. The agreement applies only to the interest and
not the loan, or principal, itself. Also at the start of the agreement the net value of the swap between the parties will be
zero. In other words both parties benefit to the same extent.

Since the swap market is so large it is usually possible for a
company seeking a swap to find a counter party with which to

make a deal. However, if it is not possible to find an exact match, but a deal can be set up where there is a net difference between the parties, then a capital sum may change hands to restore parity. Of course, while everything is equal at the start of the agreement the volatility of currency and interest rate markets ensures that things will change as time goes on!

To see how an interest rate swap can benefit both parties, before any time related distortions take place, consider two companies who both wish to borrow £500,000. One of the companies, company A, has taken out a loan with a floating interest rate of LIBOR (Loans Inter-Bank Offer Rate) plus 150 basis points - a floating rate of 7.5%, with LIBOR at 6%.

The company, however, now believes that interest rates are due to rise since inflation is starting to get out of control. The Directors therefore believe they are in for at least one if not two interest rate rises before the end of the year and could be facing up to four rises before their loan is repaid in two years time. To help manage this risk they therefore seek a swap into a fixed interest rate.

Company B on the other hand has taken out their £500,000 loan at a fixed interest rate. They, perhaps, believe interest rates have peaked and are due to fall over the next two years so they are seeking to switch into a floating interest rate repayment plan.

The two companies have a perfectly matching profile with £500,000 loans over a two year period. So they enter into an interest rate swap agreement.

Now lets say that company A could achieve a fixed interest rate of 7.7% for the same loan over a two year period. Company B on the other hand are locked into their fixed rate interest deal at 8.0% but could achieve a floating rate of LIBOR plus 230 basis points (the equivalent of 8.3%).

Interest Rates Available

	Company A	Company B	Difference
Fixed rate	7.7%	8.0%	0.3%
Floating Rate	LIBOR + 150bps	LIBOR + 230bps	80bps (0.8%)
Average difference			*0.5%*

You can immediately see that company's A credit rating must be better than that of company B. At the fixed rate company A enjoys a 0.3% advantage over company B whilst at floating rates that advantage extends to 0.8%. And it is the difference between these two advantages which can be shared between the two companies to lower their interest rate payments (that's 0.5% split two ways, or 0.25%).

Company B, currently with the fixed rate deal, agrees to pay company A's interest at LIBOR plus 150 bps. This now gives company B their required exposure to a floating interest rate.

Company A, currently with a floating rate, undertakes to pay 7.45% of company B's fixed rate interest. This now gives company A their required security of a fixed rate interest repayment plan and is calculated by taking the fixed rate they could obtain in the market of 7.7% and subtracting half of the comparative advantage discussed above which is 0.25%. Company B will still have to add 0.55% to company A's payments to meet their original 8.0% repayments.

The net outcome of this swap arrangement is shown in the table below and you can see how both companies have benefited from the deal. Company A has achieved its aims of repaying its loan through a fixed rate of 7.45% **and** this is 0.25% less than any fixed rate deal they could achieve themselves. Company B has also achieved its aims by swapping its fixed rate deal for a floating rate **and** this is the equivalent of 25 basis points or 0.25% lower than the floating interest rates they were being offered.

	Company A	Company B
Debt issued at	LIBOR + 150bps	8.0%
Company receives from other party	LIBOR + 150bps	7.45%
Company pays to other party	7.45%	LIBOR + 150bps
Company pays to original debt (top up)	Nil	0.55%
Saving over debt issued directly	0.25%	0.25%

This sort of straight forward deal is often called a "**plain vanilla swap**".

You should note, of course, that setting up such a long term contract over two years or more brings with it its own set of risks. The largest of these must be the risk of one of the companies defaulting on the agreement - **default risk**. If their forecast of interest rate movements proves disastrously wrong and they find themselves paying a much higher charge than they would have faced before the swap deal, then they may fail to honour the transaction.

The second risk that both companies face is known as "**clean risk**" and is the exposure to the fact that the opposite party may not make their payments on time.

Currency swaps

These are inherently more complex than simple interest rate swaps and often include several steps between intermediaries. *It is not uncommon for one position to be covered by two or more swap agreements.* This is because exact matches are more difficult to find when different currencies in addition to interest rates are considered.

The most common route is for the company or institution requiring a currency rate swap to broker a deal which will offset as much of their currency and interest rate risk as possible as a first step. The remaining risk remains on the company or institution's books in a process known as **warehousing**, until a suitable deal can be made. This residual risk can be covered using standard exchange based instruments.

The way that any individual currency swap agreement is set up will depend on the currencies and the time interval under consideration, as will its final form. The negotiating strength of each side will also come into play but most deals follow this route:

1.   First there is an exchange of principal where new capital is raised in one currency and then swapped into a new currency at an agreed rate of exchange.

2.   There is then an exchange of interest where both parties agree to service one another's debts.

3.   Finally, when the maturity date is reached, the amount of the principal will be re-exchanged at a pre-agreed rate.

Summary

The main advantages of swap agreements are:

- ✔ Allows the cost of borrowing to be reduced,
- ✔ Allows borrowers access to new sources of money,
- ✔ Allows advantage to be taken of differences between interest rates in different markets,
- ✔ Can be customised to meet exact requirements,
- ✔ Can lock in interest rate or currency gains already made.

The main disadvantages are:

- ✘ Not subject to the control of an exchange,
- ✘ A risk of default,
- ✘ A risk that payments will not be made on the exact date that they are due,
- ✘ More complex to arrange due to the series of payments involved.

Options

The previous three chapters have shown how Forwards, Futures and Swaps can be used to help manage risk and the similarities in the way that they operate are obvious. Options on the other hand are quite different. They are a special tool which can be used to hedge against specific risk within a portfolio.

They are both highly flexible and liquid enabling a great variety of complicated position to be constructed. Indeed, it is said that the management of virtually any risk position can be achieved by using options as a basic building block.

At this point it should be noted, however, that using options to manage your specific risk requires a view on where the underlying security is heading. So, some sort of forecasting tool must have been used as a pre-cursor to any option strategy. This is slightly different to risk management strategy created using Forwards, Futures or Swaps. In these previous cases an opinion on market movement may have been used, but once the deal has been struck that opinion becomes irrelevant - since the price and delivery date are fixed at the time the contract is agreed.

Options can be used to manage risk in almost any market including equities, interest rates, currencies, commodities, cash and futures. However, in this chapter, the main emphasis will be placed on equities.

Calls and Puts

The holder of a **Call Option**, be they an individual, company or institution, has the right to buy a certain number of shares in a specified company at a fixed price on a specific day. Note that, as the name suggests, the holder has the option or the right to buy, not an obligation.

The number of shares involved depends on how many option contracts have been purchased with one contract usually being for 1,000 shares. The price at which the shares can be bought is known as the **exercise price**, and taking up your option to buy is known as **exercising your options**. The date on which you may choose to exercise your options, or not as the case may be, is known as the **expiration date** of the contracts.

Holders of **Put Options** have the right to sell a certain number of shares in a specific company at a set price on a specific day. As before, it is an option and not an obligation.

These definitions are for "**European**" call and put options. Variations do exist, which are known as "**American**" options, where the holders have the right to buy or sell on or before a specific day. These options are obviously more flexible since the holder can decide if they wish to exercise the option and when to do so. With Europeans, although you can only exercise your options on the expiration date, you do have the alternative of selling them at any time if a buyer can be found.

If you buy an options contract, whether it be a call or put, you are taking a long position in the market, so a corresponding short position must be created. In other words another individual, company or institution must agree to the terms of your contract and deliver a specified number of shares at a contracted exercise price on (or before) the expiry date. This short position holder, or seller of the option, is known as the **option writer** and is said to have written an option. The big difference between holder and the writer of the option centres around obligation. Whereas the holder has the option or the right to buy the shares at the exercise price the writer is *obliged* to sell those shares if the option is exercised.

The Value of Options

When you buy a call option you are opening a long position with the right to buy one standard contract, which is usually 1,000 shares, on a specified date. These dates will depend on which shares the options are in, and to which "cycle" those shares belong in the options market.

There are three possibilities: They can belong to the January, February or March cycles. Each cycle covers the whole year and contains four expiration dates. So an option belonging to the January cycle will have expiry dates in January, April, July and October. Whereas an option belonging to the February cycle will have expiry dates in February, May, August and November. The exact expiration date within those months is defined by the exchange on which the options are traded.

An example of an options pricing table, which can be obtained from most financial pages, may look something like this:

Closing prices of British Petroleum plc options
Underlying security price = 744p

	Calls			Puts		
	Jan	Apr	Jul	Jan	Apr	Jul
Exercise Price						
700	50	66	78	4	14	20
750	18	36	50	19	34	40

This table shows that British Petroleum options belong to the January cycle with expiration dates in January, April and July. There will also be an expiry date in October but this will not be shown in the newspaper until the January date has been passed. The prices in the table show how much one contract will cost at exercise prices of 700p and 750p in each of these three months. So the option to buy 1,000 British Petroleum shares at a price of 750p in January will cost you 18p per share or £180 (1000 x 18p). Similarly the option to sell 3,000 in BP at 700p in April will cost you 14p per share or £420 (14p x 1,000 x 3).

In this example you can see that the price of BP shares is already 744p which is greater than the exercise price listed in the table of 700p. Obviously the right to buy these shares at a price lower than their current value must carry with it a premium. The higher an underlined security rises above an exercise price the greater this premium must become. The closer it falls to the exercise price the lower the premium will fall. The difference between the current market price of a share and the exercise price is known as **intrinsic value**. So the intrinsic value of BP options with an exercise price of 700p is 44p (700 - 744). For British Petroleum options at an exercise price of 750p, however, the intrinsic value would appear to be -6p (744 - 750). But in this situation it would be foolish to exercise any options so the true intrinsic value is zero.

- Options with a positive intrinsic value are said to be **in-the-money**.
- Options with a zero intrinsic value referred to as **at-the-money**,
- Those with an "implied" intrinsic value which is negative are called **out-of-the-money**.

These intrinsic values obviously apply regardless of the expiration date. An option with an exercise price of 750p is worthless when the underlined security price is 744 whether it is January, April, July, October or any other date. On any expiration date you simply would not choose to exercise your options. So a table of intrinsic values for British Petroleum shares corresponding to the above table would look something like this:

Intrinsic Values of British Petroleum plc options
Underlying security price = 744p

	Calls			Puts		
	Jan	Apr	Jul	Jan	Apr	Jul
Exercise Price						
700	44	44	44	0	0	0
750	0	0	0	6	6	6

You can see, though, that this table of intrinsic values differs to the closing prices quoted in the newspaper. This is because options with longer to go before expiration have a **time value**. The underlying security of BP shares may move up or down in the intervening period and options which had been out-of-the-money may suddenly become in-the-money. No matter how small or large this possibility may be it does exist and must be paid for. To calculate the time values for British Petroleum options for this example, simply subtract the intrinsic value matrix from the closing price matrix:

Time Values of British Petroleum plc options
Underlying security price = 744p

		Calls			Puts	
	Jan	Apr	Jul	Jan	Apr	Jul
Exercise Price						
700	6	22	34	4	14	20
750	18	36	50	13	28	34

Three main reasons usually arise why an individual, company or institution may enter the options market. These could be:

● The holder of a portfolio is seeking to enhance his performance through gearing. Options are cheaper to buy than the underlying shares and therefore employ less capital. Yet the options price will reflect the majority of any increase in the shares price. Therefore the return on capital is improved.

● The holder of a portfolio intends to buy a certain share in the future but does not yet have sufficient capital. Here there could be a specific risk that the share price could increase significantly and the portfolio fail to benefit. Then call options would allow the portfolio manager to take advantage of the current low price and ensure himself against an expected price rise. This is known as taking a **naked position**.

- A portfolio manager may believe that a share in the portfolio has a risk of falling in price. He could then purchase put options as a way of insuring the current value of that stock in the portfolio. This is known as taking a **covered position**.

You can see quite clearly how the portfolio managers in the latter two scenarios are using options as a way of managing the specific risk in their portfolios.

The Naked Position

Consider the second of the two reasons why a portfolio manager may enter the options market. He does not own a particular share but does wish to add it to his portfolio. Unfortunately he does not have sufficient funds to buy the quantity of shares he requires. On the other hand his market analysis has forecast that the share price is about to rise.

In this situation he could buy a call option, for example British Petroleum call options for January with an exercise price of 700p. Each contract will cost the manager 50p and this represents his maximum exposure. If the underlying shares fail to rise before the expiry date he will simply choose not to exercise his options. So the maximum he can lose is 50p per contract.

If the shares rise slightly then the value of the January call will also rise. As it does so the option holders potential loss starts to decrease until there comes a point where the value of the options has balanced the premium he had to pay in the market. At this point he will have broken even. Any further rise in the value of the shares will see the portfolio manager move into profit with his options, and there is no limit on the profit that he can make. Illustrating this graphically:

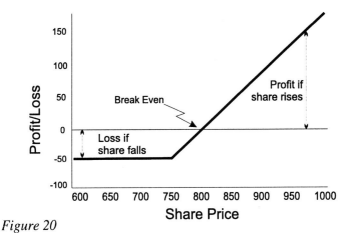

Figure 20

You can see how the right but not the obligation to buy the underlying shares has limited the portfolio manager's potential losses but left him open to large gains. A similar graph can be constructed for the situation where a portfolio manager buys put options. This is shown in Figure 21 where you can see the loss is limited to the value of the premium because the holder of the put option is not obliged to sell the shares.

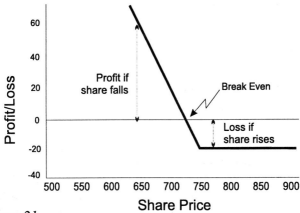

Figure 21

The opposite situation exists, of course, from the position of the options writer and Figures 22 and 23 illustrate how their positions are far more vulnerable than those of the option holder. Where an option holder knows the maximum extent of his exposure when he enters into the contract the writer can face effectively unlimited losses (though a technical limit obviously exists when a share price falls to zero).

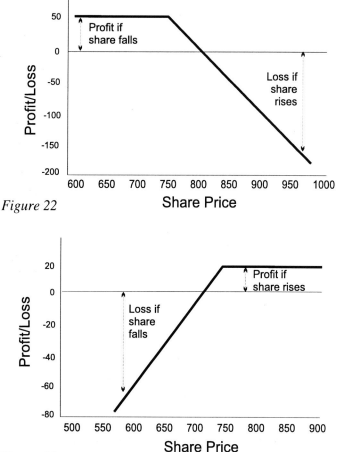

Figure 22

Figure 23

The Straddle

As indicated earlier in this chapter options can be used as building blocks in your overall risk management strategy. One of the most common combinations is known as "The Straddle". This is used where the owner of a portfolio does not hold a particular share but their forecasting techniques have shown that a share's value is about to move quite violently in one direction or the other.

The manager is not certain whether the price will rise or fall so they enter the options market and buy one call and one put option with exactly the same exercise price and expiration date. The situation is graphically illustrated in Figure 24. If these were British Petroleum options with an exercise price of 700p and expiration date in April the call options would have costs 66p per contract and the puts 14p per contract.

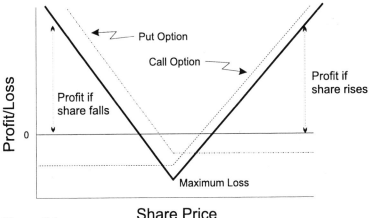

Figure 24

Now if British Petroleum shares drop significantly in value, to say 650p, then the portfolio manager would sell his put options for a higher premium than the initial 14p that he paid.

The call option, on the other hand, will be worth less than the 66p initially paid. However the market option price will still include a time value. So the manager could still sell his call option and realise a net profit, or he may alternatively hold onto the call and hope for a recovery in the share price.

Should the BP share price rise significantly, then the manager may decide to sell his call options this time for a higher premium than the 66p he paid and, as above, his put options will still be showing some time value even though they will have fallen below the 14p paid initially. So he may choose to sell his puts and walk away with an overall profit, or hold onto the puts in the belief that the share price may now retreat perhaps due to profit taking.

The Synthetic Short

In this situation a portfolio manager may have made his market forecasts and believes that a particular share price is about to go through the floor. Since he does not have any of those shares in his portfolio he cannot take advantage of the

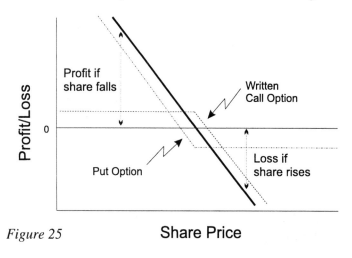

Figure 25   **Share Price**

information and sell them into the market. He is also unlikely to be able to go "short" in the shares unless he has a particularly aggressive fund owner.

In this situation the manager buys a put option and sells a call option with exactly the same exercise price and expiry date. The new combined exposure is shown in Figure 25. You can see that the overall effect is to create a short position in the shares even though none have actually been sold.

Covered Positions

Imagine that a portfolio manager has a large number of British Petroleum shares in his portfolio, and the option prices are as the example above. He has heard on the grapevine that Shell's results, which are due out in the next couple of days, will show that it has increased its overall market share to the detriment of BP. However, he also believes that some good news for BP is on its way in the form of a new exploration discovery. So he expects the BP shares in his portfolio to dip in price for a few days before then recovering.

He realises that he can take advantage of these new risks by turning to the options market. So he immediately calls up and takes a short position by selling 500 January puts in BP options at an exercise price of 700p for a consideration of 4p per contract. At the same time he opens a long position by buying 500 April puts in BP options at an exercise price of 700p for 14p per contract.

Now assume the portfolio manager was correct and the BP share price falls from 744p to, say, 720p. The January puts which he sold have no value to the buyer since the underlying security price of 720p is greater than the exercise price of 700p. So the options will not be exercised and the portfolio manager realises a profit of 4p per contract. At the same time, because the share price has fallen, the April puts are now more attractive and have an increased premium. So the Manager can sell these puts in the market for another profit of say 5p per contract. His overall profit in the options market from the fall in value of the BP shares is 500 x 1,000 x (4 + 5) = £45,000.

Should the unthinkable happen and the portfolio manager's research turn out to be erroneous the result will not be disastrous. The share price rises from 744p to 760p. The January put which the manager sold will still expire without being exercised. So he will gain 4p per contract. This time, however, the April put will have decreased in value, say to 9p per contract (though the fall will probably be less than that). This time if the portfolio manager sells his April put he will lose 5p per contract. Overall his "profit" will be given as 500 x 1,000 x (4-5) = -£5,000

You can see that it is the time value of the options which has worked in the portfolio manager's favour. A small fall in the BP share price, as predicted by the manager, would result in a reasonably large profit, whereas a rise would only result in a small loss. This is because the time value of most options only decreases rapidly close to the expiry date.

More Options

The examples of using options to manage your financial risk given in this chapter are only a few of the possibilities. You have seen how buying call or put options can limit your loss and give you potentially unlimited profits. And you have also seen in the straddle, synthetic short, and covered position examples how options with different exercise prices and expiry dates can be combined to produce the desired result.

Since there are so many possibilities of combining options they are often categorised as vertical, horizontal or diagonal strategies.

Vertical strategies involve the calls or puts with the same expiry date but different exercise prices.

	Calls		
	Jan	*Apr*	*Jul*
Exercise Price			
700	●	*66*	*78*
750	●	*36*	*50*

Horizontal strategies involve options with the same exercise price, but different expiry dates.

	Calls		
	Jan	*Apr*	*Jul*
Exercise Price			
700	●	●	●
750	*18*	*36*	*50*

And diagonal strategies involve the use of options with different exercise prices and expiry dates.

	Calls		
	Jan	*Apr*	*Jul*
Exercise Price			
700	●	*66*	*78*
750	*18*	●	*50*

When you then consider that these strategies can be extended to the use of puts as well as calls you can see the number of possibilities rise rapidly. Then, on top of all those possibilities, if you also consider the writing of calls and puts, you can see how the flexibility of the options market is so attractive.

Summary

The main advantages of exchange based options are:

- ✔ Very flexible and highly liquid market
- ✔ Limited down side risk
- ✔ Many exercise prices and expiry dates are available making it easy to create a bespoke strategy
- ✔ Regulated by an exchange.

Some the main disadvantages include:

- ✘ Volatile market
- ✘ Expensive in transaction costs
- ✘ Margin required for short positions.

Conclusion

IT WAS NOT so long ago that the main concerns of companies centred around their own management effectiveness, competition, and general economic conditions. These were the main factors that could make or break virtually any enterprise. But the rapid development of financial markets and the sophistication of the instruments available in those markets has meant that everybody needs to change their ideas. These days it is possible for any one, including individuals, to put millions of pounds (at least notionally) at risk.

Apart from the ease of entering markets there is an increased risk from the leverage which is available through derivative instruments. So, in a way, tools which are being used to manage financial risk are causing a risk themselves. Some would argue that it is not the financial tools which are causing the risk but the people who are using them, and they could have a point.

This brings up the first principle of managing financial risk, and that is an understanding of what causes it. You can never know enough about financial risk. Everyone with an interest in financial markets from the individual through to the financial institution should read as much as they can on the subject (and this will include the many individuals who do not think it applies to them, because simple decisions such as leaving a company pension scheme for a personal pension, as everyone now knows, brings with it a risk of financial loss).

Once you understand the risks that are involved with your investments and see where you could lose out monetarily you need to set about measuring those risks, and then building even the most simple model to predict how your portfolio will react in the advent of unforeseen circumstances. Markowitz showed everybody The Way by suggesting the separation of overall market risk from specific risk for individual instruments. He also helped formalise the principals of diversification as a way of managing the specific risk element of any portfolio.

With a measure of the risk you are facing and a model in place your next step is to predict as accurately as possible where market prices are heading. This can be achieved through a variety of techniques from technical analysis and charting through to analysing fundamentals and taking a consensus of views from professionals in the markets. Whichever method you choose, a forecast is vital as a pre-cursor to your choice of risk management technique.

No matter how many hours you spend on your forecasting techniques you will never be able to attain 100% accuracy. So the final step in your management of financial risk is to remove the effects of negative market movements through the use of financial instruments such as Forwards, Futures, Swaps and Options.

Unfortunately there is no such thing as a blue-print for removing financial risk from your life completely. Each individual, each company, and each financial institution will have their own aims and objectives as defined by a benchmark. However, you are taking your first step towards meeting those objectives by gaining a basic understanding of financial risk.

Unfortunately in a book of this size many important areas may have just been touched on or not even mentioned at all. For example, Value At Risk was mentioned briefly under risk modelling. A full discussion of VAR and its many uses could fill a book in itself. Also very little has been mentioned about Asset/Liability Management and the liquidity risk of dealing in the markets or the confidence levels with which risk can be modelled.

Neither has anything been mentioned about more down to earth risks such as credit risk brought about by a counter party's ability or willingness to meet its obligations. Or operations risk where human error or fraud can cause monetary loss through inadequate control of the processing, confirmation and reconciliation of transactions. Nevertheless *Understanding Financial Risk in a Day* should have given you the foundations on which to build.

Glossary

American option - An option which can be exercised on or before its expiry date.

Arbitrage - A financial transaction which generates risk free profit.

ARCH - Along with GARCH are methods of estimating future implied volatilities.

Asian option - An option whose final pay off is dependent on the average value of the underlying financial instrument over a given period.

Asset/liability management - A technique for protecting a company or institution's capital.

At-the-money - When an option's underlying value matches the exercise price.

Backwardation - When spot prices are greater than Forward prices.

Basis point - A hundredth of a percent.

Basis risk - A risk brought about by changes in spreads.

BETA - A measure of market risk.

Benchmark - A level against which the performance of an investment or portfolio is measured.

Breakout - When the value of an instrument departs from its trend lines in technical analysis.

Black-Scholes - A model for pricing financial options.

Call option - A derivative which gives the holder the right to buy an underlying financial instrument on (or before) a specific date of a pre-defined price.

Capital Asset Pricing Model - A model for valuing portfolios based upon market risk.

Covariants - A measure, statistically, of how two variables act together.

Covered position - When options and the corresponding underlying instrument are held in the same portfolio.

Credit risk - The risk that a counterparty may not meet its obligations.

Custodian - A financial institution which hold securities on behalf of investors.

Default risk - See credit risk.

Delta - A measure of an option's exposure to movement in the underlying instrument.

Derivative - A financial instrument which derives its value from the value of other instruments.

Diversification - A method of managing risk where the risk is divided among as many as possible uncorrelated exposures.

Efficient frontier - A set of portfolios where risk and reward are optimised.

Exercise price - The price given in an options contract.

Exposure - Being affected by a source of risk.

Forward - A contract to perform a specified transaction at some time in the future.

FRA - Forward Rate Agreement where the contract is linked to interest rates.

Future - Similar to a Forward but traded on an exchange.

Gamma - A second-order measure of the exposure of an option to the underlying price.

Hedge - To take off-setting risks.

Heteroscedasticity - Volatility which is not constant.

Homoscedasticity - Volatility which is constant.

Implied volatility - The volatility of an instrument calculated from its option price.

In-the-money - When an option has a positive intrinsic value.

Intrinsic value - Part of the value of an option.

Leverage - The combination and compounding of financial risks.

LIBOR - The London Inter-Bank Offered Rate is the interest rate on short term loans between banks and used as a benchmark for swaps.

Liquidity risk - The risk associated with the inability to raise cash.

Long position - When a portfolio purchases an instrument.

Margin - A cash deposit as means of collateral.

Market risk - The financial risk brought about from overall changes in the complete market.

Model risk - The risk associated with the possibility of using the wrong model.

Naked position - When a portfolio holds an option in which it does not also hold the underlying instrument.

Option - A type of derivative instrument.

OTC - Over The Counter - not traded on an exchange but tailored to meet the exact requirements of a particular customer.

Out-of-the-money - Negative intrinsic value.

Portfolio - The combination of one or many financial instruments for investment purposes.

Put option - The right to sell an underlying financial instrument on a specific date at a pre defined price.

Resistance level - A technical analysis barrier beyond which the value of a financial instrument will have difficulty reaching.

Rho - A measure of the exposure of an option to interest rates.

Risk - The exposure to an uncertainty.

Risk-free rate - A purely theoretical interest rate which an investment could earn without incurring risk. Short term treasury bonds are often used as a proxy for risk-free investments.

RSI - A technical analysis measure used to indicate if an instrument or market is over bought or over sold.

Single-scenario risk measure - A financial risk measure which is based on estimating the outcome of one possible influence or scenario.

Specific risk - Risk associated with one particular financial instrument.

Spot - The price given for immediate delivery.

Standard deviation - A measure of how far something varies from its expected or mean value.

Statistical risk measure - A risk measure which is based upon probability distributions of risk.

Stochastic - Something which evolves randomly over time.

Swap - An agreement between two parties to exchange one another's commitments, most usually with regard to interest rates or currencies, over a specified period.

Systematic risk - another term for market risk meaning risk which affects an entire group of assets or liabilities.

Theta - A measure of how an option's value changes over time.

Time value - Another component of the value of an option related to the time to expiration.

Underlying instrument - The financial instrument upon which the value of a derivative depends.

Value at risk - A measure of market risk.

Vega - Also Lambda, Kappa and Sigma. A measure of an option's exposure to changes in implied volatility.

Volatility - The standard deviation of a "random" variable.

Writer - The seller of an option contract.

The Complete Beginner's Guide to The Internet   £4.95

Everywhere you turn these days, it's Internet this, Cyberspace that and Superhighway the other. Indeed, hardly a day goes by without us being bombarded with information and reasons why you should be on the Net. But none of that is of much help in making an informed decision about joining and using the Internet.

What exactly is The Internet? Where did it come from and where is it going? And, more importantly, how can everybody take their place in this new community?

The Complete Beginner's Guide to The Internet answers all of those questions and more. On top of being an indispensable guide to the basics of Cyberspace, it is the lowest priced introduction on the market by a long way at a *surfer-friendly £4.95* (alternative books cost around £30).

Complete Beginner's Guide to Windows 95   £4.95

❑ If you've just bought a new PC it will almost certainly be running Windows 95. You may need a helping hand to get started, and this book will serve as your introduction to Windows 95.
❑ If you've decided to take the step up to Windows 95 this book will be a steadying hand to the new and to the different.
❑ If your office, school or college requires you to use a Windows 95 computer, this book will quickly show you the basics so you can get on with your work.
❑ Even if you're already using Windows 95 but simply want to do more with it, this book will teach you some neat tricks.

The Complete Beginner's Guide to Windows 95 is a low-cost, easy to understand guide, specially designed for everyone who hates wading through hundreds of pages of information to find a simple answer.

Tax Self-Assessment Made Easy   £5.99

The book tells you what you have to do and when to do it, warning you of what happens if you don't. Chapters include:
● Self-employed and the effects   ● Directors and trustees
● Record keeping requirements   ● Penalties and surcharges
● People on PAYE   ● What companies need to do.

A valuable glossary and a variety of concise appendices make this book the complete and essential guide with schedules to help you ensure that your tax bill is correct in the first place.

Understand Derivatives in a Day   £6.95

By understanding how derivatives affect apparently safe investments, such as pensions, endowment mortgages and equity plans, you can make sure your own cash is in good hands.

Nick Leeson and Co.'s dealings in the derivatives market ruined a well-respected bank. How could this possibly happen? How could a teenager run up a several hundred thousand pound debt by trading in options? And, perhaps more importantly, how do derivative traders earn their huge bonuses?

Learn...❏How private investors get started... ❏To Hedge, Straddle and control Risk... ❏Ways to limit the downside but *not* the upside... ❏About *risk free* derivative strategies... ❏Trading Psychology - Fear, Hope and Greed...   ❏Also, the History of Derivatives; Currency Speculation; Long and Short puts; Tarantula Trading; and much more.

Understand Bonds & Gilts in a Day   £6.95

This handy title shows potential investors, and those with an interest in the bond markets, how to assess the potential risks and rewards, giving a simple to follow set of criteria on which to base investment decisions. Having shown the inexperienced investor how to go about buying bonds, it also teaches even the most arithmetically shy how to calculate the yield on a bond and plan an income based portfolio. The confusing terminology used in the bond market is clearly explained with working definitions of many terms and a comprehensive glossary.